ANIMALS HEAD TO HEAD

Lion vs. Tiger

This book is dedicated to the memory of Lucy Owen,
who really cared about this series.

ISABEL THOMAS

Raintree

CHICAGO, ILLINOIS

© 2006 Raintree
Published by Raintree
a division of Reed Elsevier Inc.
Chicago, Illinois

For information, address the publisher:
Raintree, 100 N. LaSalle, Suite 1200
Chicago, IL 60602
Customer Service   888–363–4266
Visit our website at www.raintreelibrary.com

Editorial: Dan Nunn and Katie Shepherd
Design: Victoria Bevan
and Bridge Creative Services Ltd
Picture Research: Hannah Taylor
and Rebecca Sodergren
Production: Duncan Gilbert

Originated by Chroma Graphics Pte. Ltd
Printed and bound in China by
South China Printing Company

The paper used to print this book comes from
sustainable resources.

10 09 08 07 06
10 9 8 7 6 5 4 3 2 1

**Library of Congress Cataloging-in-Publiation
Data**
Thomas, Isabel, 1980-
  Lion vs. tiger / Isabel Thomas.
    p. cm. -- (Animals head to head)
  Includes bibliographical references and index.
  ISBN-13: 978-1-4109-2391-2 (library binding-
  hardcover)
  ISBN-10: 1-4109-2391-6 (library binding-hardcover)
  ISBN-13: 978-1-4109-2398-1 (pbk.)
  ISBN-10: 1-4109-2398-3 (pbk.)
  1. Lions--Juvenile literature. 2. Tigers--Juvenile
literature. I. Title. II. Title: Lion versus tiger. III.
Series: Thomas, Isabel, 1980-   Animals head to head.
  QL737.C23T47354 2005
  599.757--dc22

                         2005035251

Acknowledgments
The publishers would like to thank the following for
permission to reproduce photographs:

Corbis pp. **4 right** (Tom Brakefield), **11** (Frans
Lanting); FLPA pp. **9** (Albert Visage), **10** (Minden
Pictures/Mitsuaki Iwago), **13** (Silvestris Fotoservice),
18; Getty Images pp. **19** (Photodisc), **20** (Visuals
Unlimited); Imagestate p. **21** (Michael L. Peck);
Naturepl.com pp. **14** (T.J. Rich), **17** (Anup Shah),
22 (Bernard Castelein), **25** (Anup Shah), **26 right**
(Anup Shah); NHPA pp. **7** (Andy Rouse), **12** (Peter
& Beverley Pickford), **24** (Stephen Krasemann);
Photolibrary.com pp. **4 left** (Mike Powles), **6** (Stan
Osolinski), **8** (Mike Powles), **15** (Survival Anglia), **16**,
26 left (Animals Animals/Earth Scenes); Still Pictures
p. **29** (Pallava Bagla/UNEP).

Cover photograph of lion reproduced with
permission of Photolibrary.com/Ifa-Bilderteam
Gmbh. Cover photograph of tiger reproduced with
permission of Photolibrary.com/Bob Bennett.

Disclaimer

Contents

Any words appearing in the text in bold, **like this**, are explained in the glossary.

Meet the Big Cats

It is feeding time. In the dense Indian jungle, an enormous Bengal tiger drags his fresh kill to a hiding place. Thousands of miles away on a dusty African plain, a male lion takes the first bite of a zebra that his lionesses have just killed. No animal dares to get in his way.

Tigers and lions are both big cats, a type of **mammal**. All big cats are **predators**. This means they survive by hunting and eating other animals.

There are five types of tiger, but Bengal tigers are the most common.

Is the African lion really the king of beasts?

4

Every part of a predator's body is perfectly designed to help it find, catch, and eat meat. Strong bodies and sharp teeth make them superb fighters, too!

Man-eaters
Tigers and lions are big enough to eat humans—and some do! Lions attack roughly 100 people every year.

Bengal tigers and African lions are both fearsome hunters. But which would be crowned the champion predator? To find out, let's compare their hunting and fighting skills.

This map shows where Bengal tigers and African lions live in the wild.

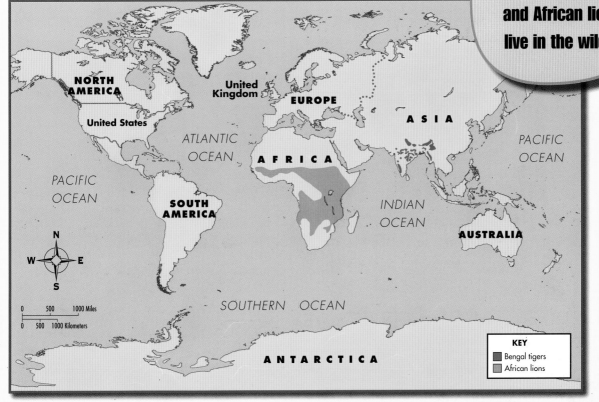

NORTH AMERICA

United Kingdom

EUROPE

ASIA

United States

ATLANTIC OCEAN

AFRICA

PACIFIC OCEAN

PACIFIC OCEAN

SOUTH AMERICA

INDIAN OCEAN

AUSTRALIA

N
W   E
S

0   500   1000 Miles
0   500   1000 Kilometers

SOUTHERN OCEAN

ANTARCTICA

KEY
Bengal tigers
African lions

5

Strength and Size

Big cats use their size and strength to hunt food and to win fights. Large animals have a much bigger choice of food because they are stronger.

Tiger power

Tigers use their huge bodies to knock **prey** over. They hunt medium-sized animals such as deer and wild pigs. But if they have the chance, tigers are strong enough to tackle crocodiles, bears, and even young elephants.

9 ft. 10 in. (3.0 m)

3 ft. 3 in. (1.0 m)

A tiger weighs as much as 50 pet cats!

A lion's pride

Most African lions live in groups called **prides**. A male lion's main job is to protect the female lions and cubs in his pride. His body is very powerful, with enormous shoulder muscles.

Lions eat medium-sized **mammals** such as wildebeest and zebras. Female lions catch most of the food for the pride. The males do not hunt unless they are living alone. They save their strength for fighting **predators** and other male lions.

A male lion's mane makes him look even bigger than he really is.

8 ft. 10 in. (2.7 m)

3 ft. 11 in. (1.2 m)

Bigger is better

A lion and tiger are almost equal in size. Tigers have longer bodies than lions, but they are not as tall.

Tigers have strong back legs to help them leap and pounce on **prey**. But a lion's body is better for fighting. Lions have more power in their shoulders and front legs. These are perfect for grabbing and pulling down an opponent.

Lions also have bigger paws. If a lion stood on this book, one paw would reach all the way across the page!

A tiger can knock down and kill an animal twice its size.

Roar power

A lion's roar is the loudest of any big cat. It can be heard up to 5 miles (8 kilometers) away. The roar tells everyone that the lion is ready to defend his **territory**!

Tigers also use booming calls to warn rivals to stay away. These terrifying sounds travel for roughly 2 miles (3 kilometers) through the tiger's jungle **habitat**. They can make prey animals stand frozen with fear.

Lions build up their muscles by fighting rivals.

HEAD TO HEAD

WINNER

	Lion	Tiger	
Size	8	8	It's an even match, shoulder to shoulder...
Strength	9	8	Lion wins by a paw and a roar!

9

The Chase

Most of the animals that big cats hunt are very fast runners. Lions and tigers need to be fast too or their meal will escape!

Fast forward

Lions can sprint at up to 30 mph (48 kph), but only in a straight line for a few seconds at a time. They give up as soon as the **prey** starts to get ahead. A hungry lion does not want to waste energy chasing something he might not catch.

In fact, a male lion finds it easier to catch a massive but slow animal, like a buffalo or a wildebeest, than a swerving gazelle!

This wildebeest wasn't fast enough to escape.

Agile tigers

Tigers have very flexible bodies and can run slightly faster than lions. They can **accelerate** from 0 to 30 mph (50 kph) in just three seconds! But, like lions, tigers are also built for short bursts of speed and do not catch everything they attack.

Powerful leg muscles make tigers excellent at jumping and climbing. They can travel up to 30 feet (9 meters) in a single leap, and climb trees with heavy prey clamped in their jaws!

A big cat's long tail helps it balance when it jumps.

Endurance

Big cats might be good at hunting, but their **prey** is good at escaping! A tiger might catch only one animal for every twenty he chases. He may have to survive for days or even weeks without food, so **endurance** is important.

Tigers need to walk long distances to find their next meal. Tough pads protect their paws from cuts and scratches.

In contrast, lions have a reputation for being lazy! They are often spotted lying around in the shade. In fact, most of their hunting takes place at night, when it is cooler. Lions rest between meals to save energy.

Big cats can eat huge amounts of meat in one sitting.

Overheated

Lions and tigers get very hot when they hunt, especially in the daytime. Tigers enjoy cooling off in water and are excellent swimmers. They can even attack any animals they come across in rivers and lakes!

A river or lake is an important part of a tiger's habitat.

HEAD TO HEAD

WINNER

	Lion	Tiger	
Speed	6	7	Tiger leaps ahead!
Endurance	7	8	Lazy male lions let females find the food.

13

A Surprise Attack!

Most **prey** animals can run very quickly, so lions and tigers have to get very close before attacking. Most **predators** use amazing skills of **stealth** to creep up on a victim. This gives it less time to escape.

Staying hidden

Clever **camouflage** helps big cats to stay out of sight as they approach their prey. A lion's sandy-colored coat blends in perfectly with the pale colors of its African **habitat**.

Camouflage helps keep animals hidden from predators and prey.

Only one thing spoils a male lion's camouflage—his big dark mane. Some **zoologists** think the stiff, wiry hair helps protect the lion in fights. Others believe it is just there to impress female lions! It shows a lion will be good at fighting and protecting his **pride**.

Confused by stripes

The bright orange coat of a tiger may look easy to spot. But most of the animals it hunts cannot see bright colors. The large stripes break up the tiger's shape. The victim cannot see a tiger in the grass until it is too late.

The tiger's striped coat blends in with its habitat.

15

Super senses

Most **predators** have sharp **senses** that help them find food and avoid enemies.

Lions use their fantastic eyesight to track down possible prey. Their large eyes can spot animals moving in the distance across the wide African plains.

Night vision

Tigers and lions can see six times better than a human in the dark. They prefer to hunt at night, when their **prey** is less likely to see them coming. When food is easy to catch, they will hunt in daylight, too.

This lioness is watching her prey from a distance as she gets ready for the chase.

Big cats have an excellent sense of smell, but they don't use it to hunt.

Big cats can also hear a much greater range of sounds than humans. They can even twist their ears around to figure out where a noise is coming from.

Helpful hairs

Whiskers are special hairs on the face that help a big cat feel its way around on dark nights. They detect tiny air movements that indicate something is moving nearby.

HEAD TO HEAD

WINNER

	Lion	Tiger	
Camouflage	7	9	Tiger's stripes leave prey confused!
Senses	9	9	Equally sharp.

Claws and Jaws

All **predators** have special weapons to help catch and kill their **prey**.

Killer claws

Big cats have razor-sharp claws that help them catch victims. When a big cat is not using his claws, he hides them away inside the paw, just like a pet cat does. This helps the claws stay super sharp.

Tigers and lions have eighteen deadly claws—five on each front foot and four on each back foot. Each claw is hooked.

When a tiger uses his claws, he can leave really deep, painful scratch marks.

18

Savage teeth

A big cat's most dangerous weapons are its amazing teeth.

Lions and tigers have 30 teeth. The biggest are the long, pointed front teeth, called **canines**. They are designed for killing and they sink deep into a victim's body.

The rest of the teeth are adapted for tearing off chunks of meat or gnawing through bone.

Even a big cat's tongue is specialized. It is tough and rough enough to scrape meat off bones!

A lion's teeth were built for eating meat!

Bite force

Tigers have extremely powerful jaws, but a lion's bite is even stronger. A lion's bite is 30 times stronger than the bite of a pet cat.

The combination of jaw power and razor-sharp teeth allows big cats to kill **prey** with a single bite.

This might be:

- a throat bite, so the victim can't breathe. This tactic is used for larger animals.
- a neck bite, so the cat's enormous teeth slice straight through the victim's **spine**.

Big cats don't chew their food— they pull off pieces and swallow them whole.

Sudden death

Making a quick kill is very important for a big cat. A long struggle would waste energy, and the **predator** might get wounded. One kick from a zebra can break a lion's jaw!

A tiger's canine teeth are the longest, at up to 3.5 inches (9 cm) long.

HEAD TO HEAD

WINNER

	Lion	Tiger	
Claws	7	7	Both are armed and dangerous.
Jaws	10	8	Lion's bite is even worse than his roar!

ROUND 5

Hunting Skills

We have seen what makes big cats such fearsome **predators**. Excellent **senses** help them to track down **prey**. When they have selected a victim, they use amazing **stealth** to sneak closer. **Camouflage** makes them almost invisible and they are great at stalking.

From about 65 feet (20 meters) away, the big cats leap forward in a burst of speed. The prey is knocked off its feet as sharp claws sink into its body. Finally, razor-like **canines** kill the prey with a single bite.

Lions learn how to fight when they are cubs.

Top predators

Lions and tigers are at the top of their food chains. Few animals would dare to try and eat them! They will hunt anything that they come across, but they prefer large **herbivores** such as deer, which make a good meal.

Most predators usually avoid hunting other **carnivores** that might fight back!

A food chain shows what eats what in a habitat.

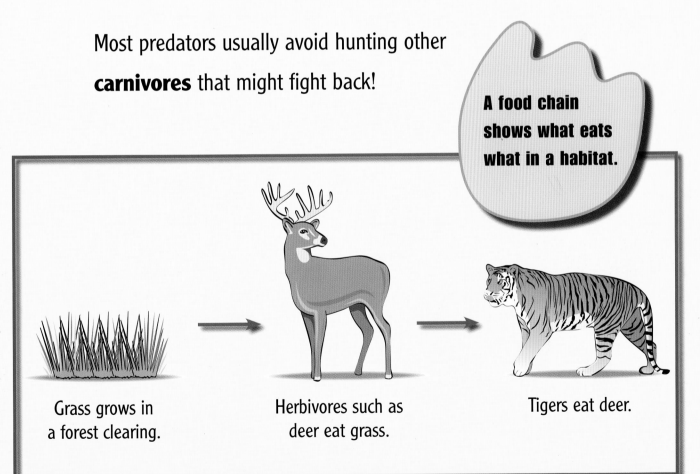

Grass grows in a forest clearing.

Herbivores such as deer eat grass.

Tigers eat deer.

Expert fighters

A lion's life is full of battles! Male lions spend most of their time trying to defend their **pride**.

Almost every day, a lion has new reasons to fight:

- to protect his pride from rival males, who would kill his cubs.
- to stop **scavengers**, like hyenas, from stealing food.
- to get the first share of meat at a kill.

Duels between male lions are ferocious and they often fight to the death. If a male gives up, he will not attract **mates** or be allowed to eat first. Only the top lions can do these things.

Males first

In return for protecting females and cubs, males expect the first share of every meal! If a younger lion tries to cut in line he risks a smack from the huge paw of a bad-tempered male!

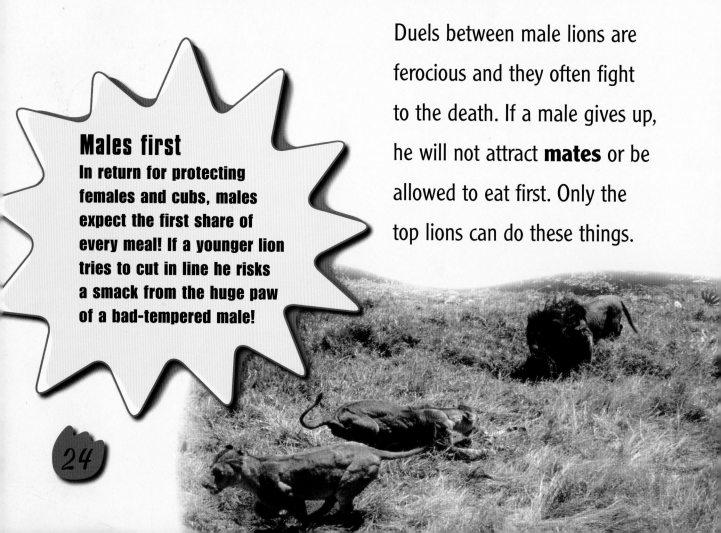

24

Peaceful tigers?

If a lion gets badly injured in a fight, he can still eat the food that the rest of his pride catches. But tigers live alone. A tiger that cannot hunt will starve, so adult tigers do not like to risk being hurt in a fight.

If male tigers do meet, they do not start fighting right away, but snarl and roar. Then they test each other's strength, standing on their back legs and wrestling until the weakest tiger gives up and runs away.

Fighting tigers box each other with their huge paws.

HEAD TO HEAD				WINNER
	Lion	Tiger		
Hunting skills	7	8	Tiger focuses on the food.	
Fighting skills	10	7	Lethal lion is a born fighter.	

Who Wins?

Amazing night vision, razor-sharp claws, bone-crunching jaws, and super strong bodies make lions and tigers fantastic **predators**—but can you decide which predator is the best? African lions and Bengal tigers would never meet in the wild. But what would happen if they did?

Battle of the big cats

They might start by snarling and roaring. If neither cat backed off, they would wrestle, standing on their back legs and boxing with their huge paws. After this test of strength, they would try to bite each other's necks, shoulders, and legs.

The big cats would be very well matched. Bengal tigers are huge, fast, and powerful hunters. But an African lion's more powerful jaws and larger head and shoulders are better for fighting.

Tigers live alone in the wild, but male lions spend their lives defending their **pride** from attack. They get much more experience of combat.

The tiger would eventually run away, realizing that the ferocious lion would never give up!

HEAD TO HEAD

	Lion	Tiger
Size	8	8
Strength	9	8
Speed	6	7
Endurance	7	8
Camouflage	7	9
Senses	9	9
Claws	7	7
Jaws	10	8
Hunting skills	7	8
Fighting skills	10	7
Total	80/100	79/100

Bow down before the lion king!

27

The Real Fight

Lions and tigers are not likely to come across each other in the wild. But there is one enemy that cannot be avoided—humans.

One hundred years ago, thousands of lions and tigers roamed the world's forests and plains. But people started to cut down forests and take land to build houses and farms. Sadly, some people started to hunt big cats for sport.

Twenty years ago there were 200,000 African lions. Now, fewer than 23,000 are left. If they are not protected, big cats will soon become **extinct**.

Lions and tigers might be fierce and strong, but they are no match for humans with guns.

Endangered species

As humans destroy more and more tiger and lion **habitats**, there is less space for the big cats to live in and less **prey** for them to eat.

Bengal tigers are already very rare. In 1900 there were roughly 100,000 tigers in the world. Scientists think there could be fewer than 5,000 left today.

Conservationists protect lions and tigers in **national parks**. But these big cats are still in danger from **poachers** who want their fur and meat. They will only survive if everyone treats them with the respect they deserve.

Some people will pay thousands of dollars for a tiger skin.

Glossary

accelerate speed up

camouflage body features that allow animals to blend into their habitat, to avoid being seen by predators or prey

canines sharp pointed teeth at the front of the mouth. Most mammals have four canines.

carnivore animal that eats mainly meat

conservationist someone who works to keep the environment safe

endurance strength and energy to survive in difficult conditions

extinct when a type of animal no longer exists

habitat place where an animal lives

herbivore animal that feeds mainly on grass and other plants

mammal animals that can make their own body heat and produce milk for their babies

mates animals that have babies together

national park large area of important land that is protected by law

poacher person who hunts or fishes animals when it is against the law

predator animal that hunts, kills, and eats other animals

prey animal that is caught, killed, and eaten by another animal as food

pride group of male and female lions that live and hunt together

scavenger animal that finds and eats dead animals instead of hunting them itself

senses ways in which an animal gets information about its surroundings

spine backbone

stealth doing something slowly and quietly to avoid being noticed

territory area that an animal lives in and defends against rivals

zoologist person who studies animals and their behavior

More Information

Books

Solway, Andrew. *Wild Predators: Killer Cats*. Chicago:
Heinemann Library, 2005.
This book explores the lives of the most dangerous big cats.

Spilsbury, Richard, and Louise Spilsbury. *A Pride of Lions*.
Chicago: Heinemann Library, 2004.
This book looks at how lions behave when they are in a group.

Spilsbury, Richard, and Louise Spilsbury. *Animals Under Threat:
Bengal Tiger*. Chicago: Heinemann Library, 2004.
Read this book to find out about the threats tigers face from humans.

Websites

www.nationalgeographic.com/kid—visit this site and search
for "lion" or "tiger" to find lots of fascinating photos and facts.

www.nwf.org/wildlife/tiger/—this site will help you to become
a tiger expert with its amazing facts and tiger history.

Sizing up the lion and tiger

This picture shows how big a male lion and tiger are, compared to a human.

Index